YIKES!
The Mystery of Energy!

by Ailynn Collins

CAPSTONE PRESS
a capstone imprint

Published by Capstone Press, an imprint of Capstone
1710 Roe Crest Drive, North Mankato, Minnesota 56003
capstonepub.com

Copyright © 2025 Hanna-Barbera.
SCOOBY-DOO and all related characters and elements
are trademarks of and © Hanna-Barbera. (s25)

Library of Congress Cataloging-in-Publication Data
is available on the Library of Congress website.

ISBN: 9798875214158 (hardcover)
ISBN: 9798875214400 (paperback)
ISBN: 9798875214417 (ebook PDF)

Summary: Get in the game as Scooby and the Mystery Inc. gang crack the case on energy. From energy's types and sources to how it can be changed and saved, uncover the remarkable science behind our ability to do work.

Editorial Credits
Editor: Christopher Harbo; Designer: Tracy Davies; Media Researcher: Svetlana Zhurkin; Production Specialist: Whitney Schaefer

Image Credits
Getty Images: Alexander Crispin, 18, Anita_Bonita, 15, Claudia Nass, 23, GoodLifeStudio, 5, Graphic_BKK1979, 16 (inset), Imago-Photo, 11 (bottom), iShootPhotosLLC, 4, KidLand, 11 (middle), LSOphoto, 9, Marilyn Nieves, 8, Martin Steinthaler, 6, milehightraveler, 22, nazar_ab, 27, nevodka, 21, pagadesign, 13 (basketball), photomaru, 24 (corn ear), studiocasper, 19 (bottom), subjug, 25, taesmileland, 19 (top); Shutterstock: Aliaksei Kaponia, 28, Ballerion, cover (explosion effect), BetsyChe, cover (lightning ball), Cartooncux (beaker), cover and throughout, HobbitArt (science icons), cover and throughout, klyaksun, cover (energy ball), lovelyday12, 26, makalex69, 24 (back), Maria Martyshova (background), cover and throughout, Photoongraphy, 29, prapass, 13 (golf ball), Sanket27, 16 (back), StockSmartStart, cover (glowing lightning)

Any additional websites and resources referenced in this book are not maintained, authorized, or sponsored by Capstone. All product and company names are trademarks™ or registered® trademarks of their respective holders.

Printed and bound in China. PO 006276

Table of Contents

INTRODUCTION
What Is Energy? 4

CHAPTER 1
Potential and Kinetic Energy 8

CHAPTER 2
Energy Transformation 14

CHAPTER 3
Energy Sources 20

CHAPTER 4
Saving Energy 26

Glossary 30
Read More 31
Internet Sites 31
Index 32
About the Author 32

What Is Energy?

What a great day to be outside! The Mystery Inc. gang has been playing an exciting game of basketball. While the rest of the gang takes a breather, Scooby keeps shooting baskets.

That's right, gang. No matter how hard we try, energy cannot be destroyed. It can be stored. It can also be transformed or changed into a different form.

But let's not get ahead of ourselves. What is energy?

Energy is everywhere. We can't see it, but we can see what it does. Energy makes things move. It powers machines and gives us heat, light, and even sound. Energy is the ability to do work or make something work.

Almost all forms of energy on Earth can be traced back to the sun. All living things need the heat, light, and even wind energy that come from the sun.

There are many forms of energy. Heat and light from the sun are forms of energy. The food we eat contains chemical energy. When you switch on the lights, electrical energy is being used. When you talk to a friend, you're using sound energy.

And that's not all! A car uses energy to travel down a road. When you walk, run, or brush your teeth, you're using energy. And when Scooby-Doo tries to lift a barbell, he's using a LOT of energy!

Wow! Energy really is everywhere! And it has so many forms. But what do they all mean?

Potential and Kinetic Energy

"You have so much potential!" Have you ever heard that phrase and wondered what it means?

Potential in this sense means that you have the ability to develop into something great in the future. In science, potential energy is the energy that is stored in an object because of its position or state. Let's look at some simple examples.

Jeepers! Look at all her potential!

Imagine you're holding a ball in your hands. As it sits there, waiting to be dropped, the ball has potential energy. Why? Because potential energy is "waiting" energy. The ball has stored energy that will get used once you drop it.

And potential energy isn't limited to objects. Your body can have potential energy too! When you sit on a couch or at the top of a slide, you are storing energy. So, it's true! You really do have a lot of potential!

I have a lot of rotential right now. Hee hee hee!

Look at the Mystery Inc. gang go! Do they have potential energy now? No! Their potential energy has changed into kinetic energy—the energy of things in motion. And the faster they move, the more kinetic energy they have.

Clearly, Scooby and his friends have a lot of kinetic energy when they run from ghosts. But the same goes for you when you ride your bike—especially downhill. You move fast because the bike has a lot of kinetic energy.

FACT

The law of conservation, or transfer, of energy says that energy doesn't disappear. It changes to a different form.

Lots of things have potential energy waiting to turn into kinetic energy. Squishy springs and stretchy slingshots are just two examples. The more they are squished or stretched, the more stored potential energy they have. When they are released, we can see their potential energy turn into kinetic energy. And the more you move, the more kinetic energy you have too!

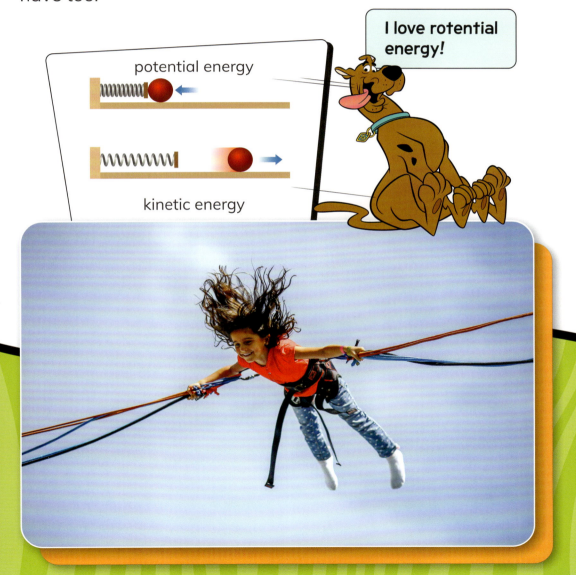

Remember how the ball in your hands has potential energy? What happens if you let it go? That's right! It drops to the ground. Why? Gravity, that's why! Gravity is the force that pulls everything toward the center of Earth.

When you let go of the ball, gravity turns potential energy into kinetic energy by pulling the ball down to the ground. Scientists have a special name for that moment before you let go. It's called gravitational potential energy.

FACT

Engineers use gravitational potential energy to build roller coasters. They calculate how much energy is needed to move the coaster's cars up, down, and around the track.

"Which has more gravitational potential renergy?"

Alright, gang! Look at Scooby holding a golf ball in one paw while holding a basketball a little higher with his other paw. Will his golf ball have a different amount of gravitational potential energy than his basketball? You bet!

Gravitational potential energy depends on how high the object is before dropping to the ground. The higher it is, the more potential energy it has. Gravitational potential energy also depends on the object's mass. Objects with more mass have more potential energy. So, Scooby's basketball, which is higher and has more mass, definitely has more potential energy than his golf ball.

CHAPTER 2
Energy Transformation

So, gang, you now know that energy is everywhere. You also know that the law of conservation says energy can't be created or destroyed. It can only be changed from one form to another.

Scientists have a term for this process of change. It's called energy transformation. But what are some common transformations that energy makes? Let's explore!

Running is one energy transformation I'm really good at!

Look at the food on your plate. Did you know that there is potential energy in it? It's called chemical potential energy.

When you eat, your digestive system breaks down food so it can be used by your body. Simply put, a chemical reaction happens and energy is released. Most of the chemical energy is transformed into kinetic energy. It gives you the ability to play and work, and it helps your cells grow. Some of the chemical energy is also changed into heat energy. This keeps your body at the right temperature.

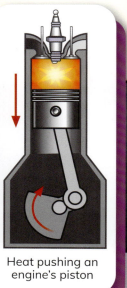

Heat pushing an engine's piston

A similar energy transformation happens in cars. The gasoline in a parked car has chemical potential energy. When the car starts, the gasoline burns, releasing heat energy.

The heat pushes the engine's pistons and changes into kinetic energy that turns the car's crankshaft. The crankshaft's rotation moves the wheels, allowing the car to move. Kinetic energy moves the car forward or backward. Vroom!

FACT

A car also transforms chemical energy into electrical energy to power its battery. The battery runs the lights, the radio, and other parts of the car.

We've learned how energy changes or transforms in our bodies and in cars. Where else can we see energy transformations?

The Mystery Inc. gang loves to make music! Their musical instruments are fun examples of energy transformations. When no one is playing them, the instruments have potential energy. Plucking guitar strings or hammering keys on a piano turn that potential energy into kinetic energy and sound energy. Playing the drums is a great way to see kinetic energy turning into very loud sound energy!

If we look around the house, we can find lots of examples of electrical energy transformations.

Many of our appliances are plugged into sockets, giving them electrical energy. When you toast bread, that electrical energy in the toaster turns into heat energy. Switching on a lamp turns electrical energy into light energy. A small amount of energy also turns into heat energy. Pushing the button on the electric kettle turns electrical energy into heat and a bit of sound energy.

Wow! There are energy transformations happening everywhere, all the time!

FACT

Chemical potential energy is also stored in batteries. When a battery is used, it releases electrical energy to light lamps, work phones, or power your computer.

Energy Transfer Experiment

WHAT YOU'LL NEED

A ruler with a groove in the middle

Four marbles

WHAT TO DO

1. Place the ruler on a flat surface like a table.
2. Set three marbles side by side in the groove in the middle of the ruler.
3. Set the fourth marble in the groove at one end of the ruler.
4. Flick the fourth marble toward the three marbles in the middle.
5. Watch what happens.

The fourth marble has potential energy. When you flick the marble, its potential energy changes to kinetic energy. This kinetic energy is then transferred from one marble to the next through collision.

Energy Sources

Okay, gang! Now that we've learned about energy types and transformations, let's look at where we get our energy. Scientists say we get energy from different sources of fuel. Fuel is anything that can be burned or changed chemically to give out energy.

If you're like Scooby and Shaggy, your favorite type of fuel is FOOD! As we've seen, food gives people and animals the energy they need to survive. But our cars, homes, and devices need fuel sources too. Let's explore some of the most common ones.

Fossil fuels—like oil and coal—are not made of dinosaurs! They're mostly formed from ancient plankton and algae.

Most of the energy we use to power things in our lives comes from fossil fuels. These fuels are made up of the remains of plants and animals that died millions of years ago. The most common forms of fossil fuels are coal, oil, and natural gas.

Coal is the black or brown rock that we burn to make electricity. Oil, which is also called petroleum, is a liquid that is made into gasoline for cars and trucks. Natural gas is—as its name implies—a gas people use to cook food and heat their homes.

Fossil fuels have given humans a lot of energy for living. But there are some big problems with these fuels. First, these sources of energy are nonrenewable. That means once they're used up, they are gone forever.

Second, burning fossil fuels is bad for the planet. They release pollution into the air we breathe and water we drink. Burning fossil fuels also releases carbon dioxide. This gas traps heat from the sun, which warms our planet and makes it harder for life to survive.

In the long term, fossil fuels are bad for our planet. So, what can we do about it?

To move away from burning fossil fuels, we need to use renewable energy sources. These sources will not run out. And they are also considered clean because they don't add more pollution to our air.

Do you remember our most important source of energy? That's right! It's the sun. Many homes today have solar panels that capture the sun's energy and turn it into electricity. Even when the sun goes down, solar energy stored in batteries can be used to light and heat our homes. And scientists are busy making better solar batteries that store energy more efficiently.

Other clean, renewable energy sources are even more down to Earth—literally! Wind farms harness the power of the wind to create electricity. Hydroelectric dams generate electricity by tapping into the power of running water. And even Earth itself gets in on the action with geothermal energy—which harnesses heat from deep within the planet.

FACT

Did you know that corn can produce energy? Corn can be turned into ethanol which can be used as a fuel to power cars and trucks.

Make Solar S'mores!

Let's use energy from the sun to make yummy s'mores!

WHAT YOU'LL NEED

duct tape
wooden skewers
pizza box
glue
aluminum foil
black paper
thermometer
cupcake liners
mini marshmallows, chocolate, and graham crackers
clear heat-proof bowl

WHAT TO DO

1. Tape the wooden skewers to the pizza box so the lid stays open.
2. Glue aluminum foil to the inside surfaces of the box and lid.
3. Place the black paper at the bottom of the pizza box.
4. Take the box outside on a hot day and face it toward the sun.
5. Use the thermometer to measure the temperature inside the box. When it reaches 158 degrees Fahrenheit (70 degrees Celsius), you're ready to cook!
6. In each cupcake liner, place a piece of chocolate and a few mini-marshmallows between two graham cracker squares.
7. Put the liners on the black paper in the box and cover them with the heat-proof bowl.
8. Keep turning the box to face the sun.
9. Once the s'mores melt, enjoy your gooey treat!

Saving Energy

Hey, gang! We've learned a lot about what energy is and where it comes from. But have you heard that it's important to save energy? It's true!

Saving or conserving energy is part of being responsible citizens and taking care of our planet. It involves using less energy to perform tasks and being careful with how we use nonrenewable energy sources. Not only does using less energy reduce pollution, but it also saves us money!

Jinkies! Who knew saving energy was as easy as riding a bike!

Shaggy asked a really good question. One easy way to save energy every day is to switch off lights when leaving a room. If no one is watching the TV, turn it off. When heating or cooling your house, close the doors to the outside to save energy.

Here are even more ideas. Hang laundry out to dry instead of using a machine. Shut the refrigerator doors tightly to save electricity. You can also walk or ride a bike to nearby places to save the energy you would have used taking a car.

Don't forget electric cars! They don't burn fossil fuels or pollute the air with exhaust.

And their batteries get better and better every year!

And that's not all! There are even bigger things we can do to save energy in our homes. We can replace old appliances with new ones that use less energy to run. We can replace old light bulbs with new LED bulbs that use less electricity. We can even upgrade old, leaky windows and add insulation to our homes to use less energy to heat and cool them.

Finally, using renewable energy to power our lives is a great solution too. By installing solar panels, we can collect energy from the sun to heat, cool, and light our homes.

FACT

Geothermal heat pumps can also heat our homes. They are three to five times more efficient than traditional heating systems.

Wow, gang, we've learned a lot about why energy is so important! Energy makes everything in our lives and our world possible.

We use it to move our bodies. We also need it to power our homes, schools, factories, and towns. And because of that, scientists are working to discover cleaner and more efficient energy sources all the time.

In the meantime, we can all do our part to use energy carefully. That way, our planet will stay healthy and keep humming along for many years to come.

GLOSSARY

algae (AL-jee)—small plants without roots or stems that grow in water or on damp surfaces

carbon dioxide (KAHR-buhn dy-AHK-syd)—a colorless, odorless gas that people and animals breathe out

collision (koh-LIH-zhuhn)—when two things run into each other

conservation (kon-sur-VAY-shuhn)—wise use of natural resources to protect them from loss or being used up

crankshaft (KRANGK-shaft)—a shaft that helps transfer power from a vehicle's engine to its wheels

fossil fuels (FAH-suhl FYOOLZ)—natural fuels formed from the remains of plants and animals; coal, oil, and natural gas are fossil fuels

geothermal (jee-oh-THUR-muhl)—relating to the intense heat inside Earth

gravity (GRAV-uh-tee)—a force that pulls objects with mass together; gravity pulls objects down toward the center of Earth

hydroelectric (hye-droh-i-LEK-trik)—to do with the production of electricity from moving water

mass (MASS)—the amount of material in an object

plankton (PLANGK-tuhn)—single-celled plants and animals that live in water and drift with currents

READ MORE

Harts, Marie. *Energy*. Buffalo, NY: Britannica Educational Publishing, 2024.

Jackson, Tom. *Forces & Motion*. Minneapolis: Bearport Publishing Company, 2025.

Turner, Myra Faye. *Discovering Forces and Motion in Max Axiom's Lab*. North Mankato, MN: Capstone Press, 2025.

INTERNET SITES

Cool Kid Facts: Kinetic Energy Facts
coolkidfacts.com/kinetic-energy

Mighty Owl Science: Renewable vs. Nonrenewable Resources
youtube.com/watch?v=jwzupl9pf6Y

Next Generation Science: Energy Transformations
youtube.com/watch?v=PKm4ZVNmJyQ

INDEX

chemical energy, 6, 15, 16, 18

electrical energy, 6, 16, 18

energy transformation, 4, 5, 10–13, 14–18

food, 6, 15, 20

fossil fuels, 21–23, 28

geothermal energy, 24, 28

gravitational potential energy, 12–13

heat energy, 5, 6, 15, 16, 18, 22

hydroelectric energy, 24

kinetic energy, 10–12, 15, 16, 17

light energy, 5, 6, 18

potential energy, 8–13, 15, 16, 17, 18

saving energy, 26–28

solar energy, 23, 28

sound energy, 5, 6, 17, 18

sun, 6, 22, 23, 28

wind energy, 6, 24

ABOUT THE AUTHOR

Ailynn Collins has written many books for children, from stories about aliens and monsters, to books about science, space, and the future. These are her favorite subjects. She lives outside Seattle with her family and five dogs. When she's not writing, she enjoys participating in dog shows and dog sports.